My Year
IN THE
BIBLE
a memory Journal

HARVEST HOUSE PUBLISHERS
EUGENE, OREGON

MY YEAR IN THE BIBLE

Text copyright © 2017 Terry Glaspey
Planner copyright © 2017 Harvest House Publishers
Published by Harvest House Publishers
Eugene, Oregon 97402
www.harvesthousepublishers.com

ISBN 978-0-7369-7109-6 (pbk.)

Printed in the United States of America

18 19 20 21 22 23 24 25 / ML-JC / 10 9 8 7 6 5 4 3 2

An Invitation to Journal the Journey

The Bible is the book that almost everyone admires. It is the book that believers build their lives around. It is the book that has shaped so much of what is good in our world. And it is also the book that few people actually spend very much time reading. If they do read the Bible, for many it is mostly a matter of revisiting their favorite parts and neglecting the rest. But if we believe that this book is truly God's Word, then doesn't all of it deserve our attention? That's where this journal comes in. It is a helpful tool for undertaking an adventure of reading the whole Bible: every book...every page...every verse.

To encourage you in this adventure, we have organized it as a 365-day journey through the Bible. Whether you manage to do all 365 days in one calendar year, or you set a goal of reading five days a week, or whatever other way you decide to make use of it, this book is meant to be about *your* journey—taken at a pace that works for you and providing an opportunity to reflect along the way on what it means for you.

Each of the readings will take 10 to 15 minutes on average. Because the Bible is a big book, we are purposely moving through it quickly, as there is a lot of territory to cover. Hopefully, this reading plan will help you in two ways: 1) to get a better handle on the big picture of the story of how God continues to make Himself known to His people, and 2) to let Scripture impact your life in practical and powerful ways.

Once you have done the reading, then it is up to you to decide how to use the blank space provided. The only "rule" is to do something that is meaningful to you as you create an ongoing record of your adventure in God's Word. You might want to write a summary of what you learned from what you've read. You might want to write out a verse that stood out to you. Maybe you'll decide to jot down a personal prayer inspired by the relevant Scripture passage. Or if you are creatively inclined, you might want to sketch or color or doodle in the space. Whatever you do with the space is up to you, but if you fill it in, you'll be creating a keepsake for the future, a reminder of how you were inspired by your Bible reading journal. And the great thing is that this kind of engagement means you are more likely to remember what you read and apply it to your life.

We have also included a few maps and charts to help give some context to the unfolding biblical narrative, and there are short introductions to each book of the Bible to provide a few pointers on themes to look for. These are meant to help you understand how each part of Scripture is a piece of the whole big story, which is ultimately a story of love, grace, and redemption.

Whether you do this on your own or with a group of friends, I pray that you will enjoy and be inspired by your "year in the Bible"!

Introduction to the Book of Genesis

We begin our year through the Bible at the beginning. Genesis is the book of beginnings, a book that provides answers for the big questions people have always asked: *Where did we come from? Why are we here? Why is there so much evil and suffering in the world?* Genesis does not answer these questions in the way we'd usually expect—through some sort of philosophical or theological discourse—but rather through the telling of stories about God's relationship with His people. Here we find the story of creation, of the fall, of Noah and the great flood, and the stories of Abraham, Isaac, Jacob, and Joseph. This is the beginning of the story of God's plan to redeem humanity. And what a story it is!

Day 1   Read Genesis 1–3

Day 2   Read Genesis 4–7

Day 3   Read Genesis 8–11

The Biblical World

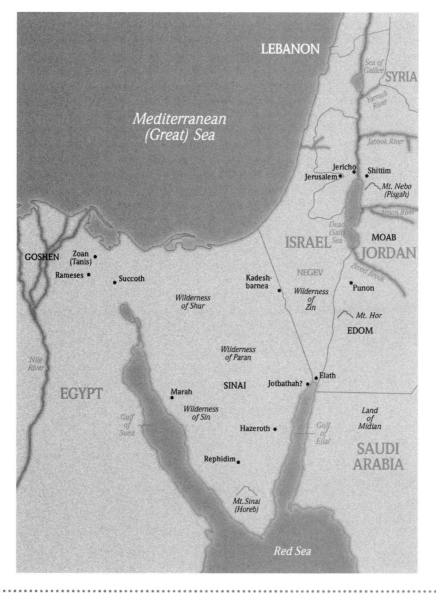

LEBANON

SYRIA

Sea of Galilee

Yarmuk River

Jabbok River

Mediterranean (Great) Sea

Jericho •
• Shittim
Jerusalem •
Mt. Nebo (Pisgah)

Arnon River

Dead (Salt) Sea

ISRAEL

MOAB

JORDAN

GOSHEN
Zoan (Tanis) •

NEGEV

Zered Brook

Rameses •
• Succoth

Kadesh-barnea •
Wilderness of Zin
• Punon

Wilderness of Shur

Mt. Hor

EDOM

Wilderness of Paran

Nile River

EGYPT

Wilderness of Sin
SINAI
Jotbathah? •
• Elath

Marah •

Gulf of Suez

Hazeroth •

Gulf of Eilat

Land of Midian

SAUDI ARABIA

Rephidim •

Mt. Sinai (Horeb)

Red Sea

Day 4   Read Genesis 12–14

Day 5   Read Genesis 15–17

Day 6   Read Genesis 18–20

Day 7   Read Genesis 21–23

Day 8   Read Genesis 24–25

Day 9   Read Genesis 26–28

Day 10   Read Genesis 29–30

Day 11   Read Genesis 31–32

Day 12   Read Genesis 33–35

Day 13   Read Genesis 36–38

Day 14   Read Genesis 39–41

Day 15   Read Genesis 42–44

Day 16   Read Genesis 45–47

Day 17   Read Genesis 48–50

Introduction to the Book of Exodus

By the conclusion of the book of Genesis, the chosen people are in Egypt, and over time they eventually become captives, slaves of the Egyptians. But God has not forgotten His children, and He will bring them out of slavery into freedom. Exodus is a story about redemption that gives hope to all those who are downtrodden. In this book, Moses obeys a call from God to lead His people out of captivity and to Mt. Sinai. There God gives them the Law—instructions for how they are to live as the chosen people of God.

Day 18   Read Exodus 1–3

Day 19   Read Exodus 4–6

Day 20   Read Exodus 7–9

Day 21   Read Exodus 10–12

Day 22   Read Exodus 13–15

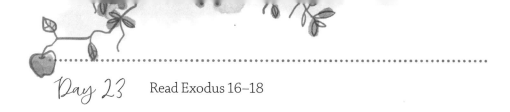

Day 23   Read Exodus 16–18

Day 24   Read Exodus 19–21

Day 25   Read Exodus 22–24

Day 26   Read Exodus 25–27

Day 27   Read Exodus 28–29

Day 28   Read Exodus 30–32

Day 29   Read Exodus 33–35

The Tabernacle

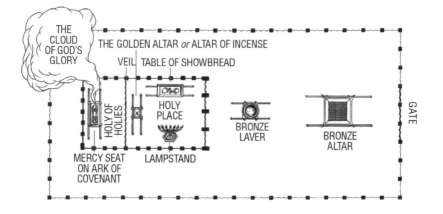

THE CLOUD OF GOD'S GLORY

THE GOLDEN ALTAR *or* ALTAR OF INCENSE

VEIL   TABLE OF SHOWBREAD

HOLY OF HOLIES

HOLY PLACE

BRONZE LAVER

BRONZE ALTAR

GATE

MERCY SEAT ON ARK OF COVENANT

LAMPSTAND

Day 30   Read Exodus 36–38

Day 31   Read Exodus 39–40

Introduction to the Book of Leviticus

With Leviticus, we turn to the "rule book" of the Old Testament. And let's be honest. It doesn't have the same great stories as Genesis and Exodus. But Leviticus serves an important function. It is filled with advice and regulations on how to live a holy life and how to worship God.

In addition to the expected laws about morality, this book deals with the system of offerings, ritual purity, and the priesthood. Along the way, there are guidelines for what to eat, what to do about skin disease, how to treat the poor and needy, and much more. Some of the laws seem strange to us today, but in the context of the time, they helped people lead lives of health and harmony.

Day 32   Read Leviticus 1–4

Day 33   Read Leviticus 5–7

Day 34   Read Leviticus 8–9

Day 35   Read Leviticus 10–12

Day 36   Read Leviticus 13–15

Day 37   Read Leviticus 16–18

Day 38   Read Leviticus 19–21

THE FEASTS OF THE OLD TESTAMENT

Passover: A remembrance of when the Lord "passed over" Jewish homes marked with the blood of a lamb during the last plague on Egypt (Exodus 12). A reminder that God has redeemed us from sin.

The Feast of Unleavened Bread: Occurs immediately after Passover to remember when the Israelites ate bread with no yeast because of their haste in preparing to leave Egypt. A reminder of leaving sin behind.

The Feast of Firstfruits: Takes place at the beginning of harvest, an offering of the first grain of the crop to God. A reminder of our dependence upon God as provider.

The Feast of Weeks: Occurs 50 days after Firstfruits and celebrates the end of the grain harvest. Called *Pentecost* in the Greek language. A reminder of gratitude for the harvest.

The Feast of Trumpets: Held on the first day of the seventh month of the Jewish calendar. They used trumpets (Numbers 29:1) to mark the end of the agricultural year and the entry into the "sacred season." A reminder to be prepared.

The Day of Atonement: Takes place ten days after the Feast of Trumpets. It was the day when the High Priest would enter the Holy of Holies to make an offering for the sins of the people. A reminder of God's mercy and forgiveness.

The Feast of Tabernacles: Takes place five days after the Day of Atonement. For seven days the Jewish people live in booths to recall their sojourn in the land of Canaan. A reminder of God's deliverance and faithfulness.

Day 39   Read Leviticus 22–23

Day 40   Read Leviticus 24–25

Introduction to the Book of Numbers

Unless you are someone who is fascinated by numbers, you might find this book to be a bit tedious. A lot of counting happens in these pages; it's a sort of biblical census. But that's not all. In a sense, you can think of this book as the story of Plan B, the years of wandering in the wilderness brought on by Israel's disobedience. The chosen ones are on their way to the promised land, but there are many struggles along the path.

Day 42   Read Numbers 1–2

Day 43   Read Numbers 3–4

Day 44   Read Numbers 5–7

Day 45   Read Numbers 8–10

Day 46   Read Numbers 11–13

Day 47   Read Numbers 14–15

Day 48   Read Numbers 16–18

Day 49   Read Numbers 19–21

Day 50   Read Numbers 22–24

Day 51   Read Numbers 25–26

Day 52   Read Numbers 27–29

Day 53   Read Numbers 30–31

Day 54   Read Numbers 32–33

Day 55   Read Numbers 34–36

Introduction to the Book of Deuteronomy

Deuteronomy is essentially the transcription of Moses' farewell sermons, his last words to his people before his death. Because he will not be entering the promised land with them, Moses wishes to remind them of their covenant relationship with God. Due to who they have become and what He has promised them through the covenant, the Lord requires nothing less than complete allegiance. Deuteronomy emphasizes the idea that God's laws are the result of God's love—a gift for our own good.

Day 56   Read Deuteronomy 1–2

Day 57   Read Deuteronomy 3–4

Day 58   Read Deuteronomy 5–7

HOW SHOULD WE THINK ABOUT THE LAW?

A significant portion of the first books of the Old Testament is made up of the laws given to God's people. Between Exodus 20 and the end of Deuteronomy, more than 600 commands are given for how God's people are to live. Some of them concern personal morality, and some have to do with regulations concerning worship and rituals. While Jesus says that He has "fulfilled" the Law (Matthew 5:17), it still is important for what it reveals about God: that He is holy and wants us to be holy, that He makes provision for forgiveness (the sacrifices point toward Jesus' sacrifice), and that He is concerned with even the practical matters of our lives—take for example the health and dietary laws. Paul says in Galatians 3:24 that the Law is our tutor, leading us toward Christ, and that love is the fulfillment of the Law (Romans 13:10).

Day 60   Read Deuteronomy 11–13

Day 61   Read Deuteronomy 14–17

Day 62   Read Deuteronomy 18–20

Day 63   Read Deuteronomy 21–23

Day 64   Read Deuteronomy 24–26

Day 65   Read Deuteronomy 27–28

Day 66   Read Deuteronomy 29–31

Day 67   Read Deuteronomy 32–34

Introduction to the Book of Joshua

After all their years of wandering, the Israelites are finally able to enter into the promised land. However, before they can claim what God has promised them, they must wage battles against a number of enemies. This is a book of violence and high drama as the land is taken, piece by piece, under the leadership of Joshua. Once they have taken the land, it is divided between the twelve tribes of Israel.

Day 68   Read Joshua 1–4

Day 69   Read Joshua 5–7

Day 70   Read Joshua 8–9

Day 71   Read Joshua 10–11

Day 72   Read Joshua 12–14

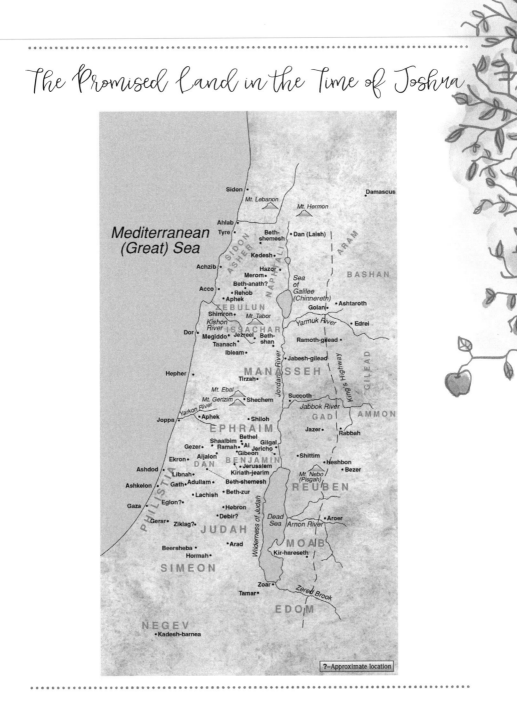

Day 73   Read Joshua 15–17

Day 74   Read Joshua 18–20

Day 75 Read Joshua 21–22

Day 76 Read Joshua 23–24

Introduction to the Book of Judges

Judges contains some great stories, but it is generally a pretty depressing read. Following the death of Joshua, God raises up a series of judges to rule the land. A cyclical pattern emerges: Over and over again the people disobey God and bring violence and shame upon their land. The recurring phrase is "everyone did what was right in their own eyes." They selfishly follow their own path, a path which leads to defeat and destruction rather than to what God has in mind for them. Then, when they cry out for help He sends a new judge to rescue them, and in time the cycle starts again. Judges is a testimony to the infinite patience of God. He continued to send new leaders for the people even though they made the same mistakes again and again.

Day 77   Read Judges 1–3

Day 78   Read Judges 4–6

Day 79   Read Judges 7–8

Day 80   Read Judges 9–10

Day 81   Read Judges 11–13

Day 82   Read Judges 14–16

Day 83   Read Judges 17–19

Introduction to the Book of Ruth

After all the violence and disobedience recorded in Judges, the book of Ruth is a breath of fresh air, a gentle tale of love and redemption. It is interesting that Ruth, the heroine of this story, is not an Israelite, but a Moabite—a member of one of the nations that was an enemy of Israel. This adds even more poignancy to this unforgettable story of friendship, loyalty, kindness, and real love.

Introduction to the Book of 1 Samuel

First Samuel deals with the beginnings of the Israelite monarchy. It revolves around three men: Samuel, the faithful prophet; Saul, the troubled and often disobedient first king; and David, Saul's successor. Up to this time, God was considered to be Israel's only "king," but now the people were clamoring for a human king. In a time of great national disaster, Samuel calls for spiritual renewal, and despite the warnings God had given, the people demand a king. Saul, appointed to that position, is a failure. But in his last great act as God's prophet, Samuel anoints David, a young shepherd boy, to be the successor. The tense situation between Saul and David unfolds in this dramatic book.

Day 86   Read 1 Samuel 1–3

Day 87   Read 1 Samuel 4–7

Day 88   Read 1 Samuel 8–10

Day 89   Read 1 Samuel 11–13

Day 90　　Read 1 Samuel 14–15

Day 91　　Read 1 Samuel 16–17

Day 92 Read 1 Samuel 18–20

Day 93 Read 1 Samuel 21–24

Day 94   Read 1 Samuel 25–27

Day 95   Read 1 Samuel 28–31

Introduction to the Book of 2 Samuel

The story of the early Israelite monarchy continues with David's reign following the death of Saul. At first highly successful, David manages to unite all of Israel under his rule and establishes Jerusalem as the capital. His own moral failures come to the forefront when he becomes involved with Bathsheba. Later, he nearly loses his throne in a plot hatched by his own son Absalom.

Day 96   Read 2 Samuel 1–3

Day 97   Read 2 Samuel 4–7

Day 98   Read 2 Samuel 8–11

Day 99   Read 2 Samuel 12–13

Day 100   Read 2 Samuel 14–15

Day 101   Read 2 Samuel 16–17

Day 102   Read 2 Samuel 18–19

Day 103   Read 2 Samuel 20–22

Day 104   Read 2 Samuel 23–24

Introduction to the Book of 1 Kings

First Kings was most likely written during the exile of Israel in Babylon to answer some nagging questions: What went wrong? How did Israel plummet from the good years it knew with kings David and Solomon to the despair that followed as the nation became enslaved in a foreign land? The book begins with the death of David and chronicles the reign of his son Solomon. We see Solomon building the temple and expanding the power of the nation. Though usually known for his wisdom, Solomon fails to show much of it when choosing his wives. Several of them come from the neighboring nations where idolatry is practiced, and this affects the moral course of Israel itself. When Solomon dies, the nation is divided into two kingdoms.

Day 105   Read 1 Kings 1–3

Day 106   Read 1 Kings 4–6

Day 107   Read 1 Kings 7–8

Day 108   Read 1 Kings 9–10

Day 109   Read 1 Kings 11–12

Day 110   Read 1 Kings 13–14

Day 111   Read 1 Kings 15–17

The Divided Kingdom

931-586 B.C.

Following the reign of Solomon, the Jewish people are divided into two kingdoms—Israel in the north and Judah in the south. Each has its own king, and each is visited by God's prophets. Eventually both kingdoms prove unfaithful and are taken into captivity in Babylon.

Day 112   Read 1 Kings 18–19

Day 113 Read 1 Kings 20–22

Introduction to the Book of 2 Kings

Originally part of the same scroll as First Kings, this book continues the unfortunate story of the decline and fall of God's chosen people. Despite a few bright years of repentance and spiritual renewal under King Josiah, first Israel and then Judah spiral downward into idolatry under the rule of evil kings. The book ends with the eventual destruction of both Israel and Judah, and the exile and captivity in Babylon.

Day 114   Read 2 Kings 1–2

Day 115   Read 2 Kings 3–4

Day 116   Read 2 Kings 5–7

Day 117   Read 2 Kings 8–9

Day 118   Read 2 Kings 10–12

Day 119   Read 2 Kings 13–14

Day 120   Read 2 Kings 15–16

Day 121   Read 2 Kings 17–18

Day 122   Read 2 Kings 19–21

Day 123   Read 2 Kings 22–25

Introduction to the Book of 1 Chronicles

Most likely written just after the Israelites' return from captivity, First Chronicles tells the same stories as Second Samuel—think of them as coming from a different "camera angle." Here the emphasis is placed more on the religious history than the political history. Much of the focus is on David's line and the southern kingdom of Judah. As such, it is a somewhat more sanitized version, offering a generally positive spin on the events and people involved. The chronicler, probably intending to unite the returning exiles with a more hopeful spin on their past, omits the stories that demonstrate David's failings.

Day 124   Read 1 Chronicles 1–3

....

Day 125   Read 1 Chronicles 4–6

....

Day 126   Read 1 Chronicles 7–9

....

Day 127   Read 1 Chronicles 10–12

Day 128   Read 1 Chronicles 13–16

Day 129   Read 1 Chronicles 17–19

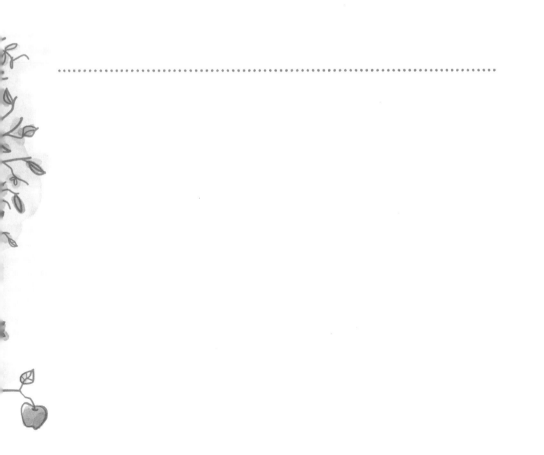

A Chart of the Kings and Prophets of Israel and Judah

(Dates are approximate and represent the general consensus.)

Date (BC)	Kings of Judah	Prophets	Kings of Israel
975	1. Rehoboam, 17 years	Ahijah	1. Jeroboam, 22 years
958	2. Abijah, 3 years	Shemaiah	
955	3. Asa, 41 years	Azariah	
954			2. Nadab, 2 years
953		Hanani	3. Baasha, 24 years
930		Jehu	4. Elah, 2 years
929			5. Zimri, 7 days
929			6. Omri, 12 years
918		Elijah	7. Ahab, 22 years
914	4. Jehoshaphat, 25 years	Micaiah	
897		Elisha	8. Ahaziah, 2 years
896		Jahaziel	9. Jehoram, 12 years
892	5. Jehoram, 8 years		
885	6. Ahaziah, 1 year		
884	Athaliah, 7 years*	Jehoiada	10. Jehu, 28 years
878	7. Joash, 40 years		
856		Jonah	11. Jehoahaz, 17 years
839	8. Amaziah, 29 years		12. Jehoash, 16 years
825		Hosea	13. Jeroboam II, 41 years

* She usurped the throne and is not considered a legal ruler.

Date (BC)	Kings of Judah	Prophets	Kings of Israel
810	9. Uzziah, 52 years	Joel	Interregnum, 11 years
784		Amos	14. Zechariah, 6 months
772			15. Shallum, 1 month
771			16. Menahem, 10 years
760			17. Pekahiah, 2 years
758			18. Pekah, 20 years
757	10. Jotham, 16 years		
741	11. Ahaz, 16 years	Obed	
730		Isaiah	19. Hoshea, 9 years
726	12. Hezekiah, 29 years	Micah	
721		Nahum	Captivity of Israel
697	13. Manasseh, 55 years	Habakkuk	
642	14. Amon, 2 years		
640	15. Josiah, 31 years	Jeremiah	
609	16. Jehoahaz, 3 months	Zephaniah	
609	17. Jehoiakim, 11 years		
606	First Captivity of Judah	Ezekiel and Daniel	
598	18. Jehoiachin, 3 months		
598	Second Captivity of Judah		
586	Last Captivity of Judah		
536	Return of Jewish Captives		
516	Temple Restored	Zechariah and Haggai	

Day 130   Read 1 Chronicles 20–23

Day 131   Read 1 Chronicles 24–26

Introduction to the Book of 2 Chronicles

Second Chronicles continues the story of the Davidic monarchy by recording Solomon's triumphant architectural project: building the temple. The writer, however, cannot ignore Judah's many evil kings and how their idolatry and wickedness led to the fall of David's kingdom, so he includes these stories as well.

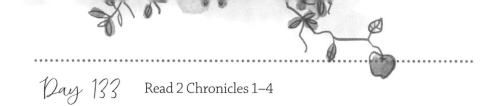

Day 133   Read 2 Chronicles 1–4

Day 134   Read 2 Chronicles 5–7

Day 135   Read 2 Chronicles 8–10

Day 136   Read 2 Chronicles 11–14

Day 137   Read 2 Chronicles 15–18

Day 138   Read 2 Chronicles 19–22

Day 139   Read 2 Chronicles 23–25

Day 140   Read 2 Chronicles 26–28

Day 141   Read 2 Chronicles 29–30

Day 142   Read 2 Chronicles 31–33

Introduction to the Book of Ezra

Ezra tells the story of the return of God's people from exile in Babylon. Under Zerubbabel's leadership, a fairly modest contingent returns and begins rebuilding the temple in Jerusalem. Then Ezra, a priest, returns with a much larger group and restores worship in the temple.

....

Day 144   Read Ezra 1–2

....

Day 145   Read Ezra 3–5

....

Day 146   Read Ezra 6–8

Day 147   Read Ezra 9–10

Introduction to the Book of Nehemiah

Nehemiah continues the story of the return from exile some twelve years after the end of the book of Ezra. Nehemiah, a man of prayer, leads the people in restoring social justice and spiritual commitment. He guides them in rebuilding the walls of Jerusalem. After a national revival spurred by the reading of God's Law, the people resettle the land.

Day 148   Read Nehemiah 1–3

Day 149   Read Nehemiah 4–6

Day 150   Read Nehemiah 7–8

Day 151   Read Nehemiah 9–10

Day 152   Read Nehemiah 11–13

Introduction to the Book of Esther

Although God is not mentioned by name even once in the entire book of Esther, He is obviously operating behind the scenes to strengthen the resolve of Esther, a woman who uses integrity and intelligence to save her nation. It is a story of court intrigue and evil machinations with lots of danger and suspense. And it is the story of the origin of the feast of Purim, the only non-Mosaic feast in the Jewish calendar. (The story probably takes place during the time period covered by the book of Ezra.)

Day 153   Read Esther 1–3

Day 154   Read Esther 4–7

Day 155   Read Esther 8–10

Introduction to the Book of Job

With Job we begin the section of Old Testament books commonly known as the Wisdom Books. We don't know much about the historical setting of Job, but we do know that it is a brutally honest poetic examination of the problem of suffering. If you look to the book for an answer to the problem of evil, you'll probably find it unsatisfactory. In fact, much of the book seems focused on unmasking the inadequacy of simplistic theological answers, as seen in the words of Job's friends, who try to help him understand why such a great tragedy has befallen him. Instead, the only answer to the question "why?" seems to be that we will never understand the mystery and must trust in God's wisdom and power. Ultimately, the act of God speaking to Job seems answer enough for the humbled sufferer.

Day 156   Read Job 1–5

Day 157   Read Job 6–10

Day 158   Read Job 11–15

Day 159   Read Job 16–21

Day 160   Read Job 22–28

Day 161   Read Job 29–33

Day 162   Read Job 34–37

Introduction to the Book of Psalms

Psalms is the songbook of the Bible, a collection of unforgettable hymns and songs by David, Moses, and other writers. It has been used in Jewish and Christian worship throughout the ages because the psalmists put the feelings of God's people into words so well. There is a psalm to fit just about any mood one might be experiencing: awestruck reverence, impatience with God, anger and fear regarding your enemies, thankfulness, and cries for help. The book of Psalms is filled with raw human emotion and beautiful poetic expression. For this reason, it is a favorite for many Bible readers.

Day 164   Read Psalms 1–5

Day 165   Read Psalms 6–12

Day 166   Read Psalms 13–17

Day 167   Read Psalms 18–22

Day 168   Read Psalms 23–30

Day 169   Read Psalms 31–37

A PSALM FOR EVERY SEASON: THE AMAZING VARIETY IN THE PSALMS

Though every psalm is unique, there are several categories into which they tend to fall. Each of these kinds of psalms has its own form and pattern and exists for a particular purpose. Each is useful for expressing a different kind of emotion or for offering a different kind of prayer to God. You might find it helpful as you read through them to try to identify what category each falls into.

Hymns: These psalms are simple songs of praise to God.
Examples: Psalms 8, 33, 66, 103, 148

Lament Psalms: These express sadness and deal with the pain of life, calling for God to act on our behalf.
Examples: Psalms 3, 7, 25, 44, 55, 80, 123

Imprecatory Psalms: These call for God's justice and intervention against our enemies.
Examples: Psalms 35, 69, 88, 109, 140

Thanksgiving Psalms: These express thanks to God for what He has done.
Examples: Psalms 30, 32, 34, 67, 100, 124

Wisdom Psalms: These are "teaching" psalms, expounding on the way of wisdom.
Examples: Psalms 1, 37, 49, 73, 128

Royal Psalms: These were written to be used in the presence of kings and dignitaries.
Examples: Psalms 18, 29, 45, 93, 99

Songs of Ascent: These psalms were sung by worshippers on their way up to Jerusalem.
Examples: Psalms 120–134

Day 170   Read Psalms 38–44

Day 171   Read Psalms 45–51

Day 172   Read Psalms 52–59

Day 173   Read Psalms 60–67

Day 174   Read Psalms 68–71

Day 175   Read Psalms 72–77

Day 176   Read Psalms 78–81

Day 177   Read Psalms 82–89

Day 178   Read Psalms 90–97

Day 179   Read Psalms 98–104

Day 180   Read Psalms 105–107

Day 181   Read Psalms 108–116

Day 182   Read Psalms 117–118

Day 183   Read Psalm 119

Day 184   Read Psalms 120–133

Day 185   Read Psalms 134–142

Day 186   Read Psalms 143–150

Introduction to the Book of Proverbs

Proverbs is a collection of wise sayings by Solomon and others. It contains practical advice in memorable, bite-size snippets on such topics as the need for wisdom, the danger of bad companions, compassion toward the needy, the dangers posed by the tongue, the hazards of sexual immorality, and the foolishness of the lazy. Its overall theme is this: The fear of the Lord is the beginning of wisdom.

Day 187   Read Proverbs 1–4

Day 188   Read Proverbs 5–8

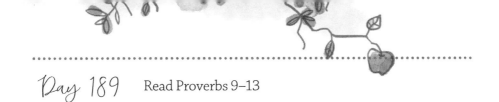

Day 189   Read Proverbs 9–13

Day 190   Read Proverbs 14–17

Day 191   Read Proverbs 18–21

Day 192   Read Proverbs 22–24

Day 193   Read Proverbs 25–28

Day 194   Read Proverbs 29–31

Introduction to the Book of Ecclesiastes

Ecclesiastes confirms that being a person of faith does not always mean being a positive thinker! This book is an honest and open-eyed philosophical reflection on life...and the conclusions are pretty negative. Everywhere the author looks he sees examples of life's apparent lack of meaning—inequality and unfairness, religious hypocrisy, and the uncertainty of the future. But under all the vanity resides a deeper truth: A life lived with and for God gives us meaning, wisdom, and purpose, even if it doesn't guarantee that everything is always going to come up roses.

Day 195   Read Ecclesiastes 1–6

Introduction to the Song of Solomon

Those prudish folks who equate sin with sexuality may be surprised to find this book in the Bible. It is an unabashed and earthy celebration of romance, filled with two lovers' poetic descriptions of their longing and unquenchable desire for one another. Here we see the joy of faithful love as God originally intended it! Some have also seen this poem as an allegory of God's love for Israel and Christ's love for the church. It can certainly be read that way, but don't miss recognizing how it celebrates love between a man and a woman.

Day 197   Read Song of Solomon 1–4

Day 198   Read Song of Solomon 5–8

Introduction to the Book of Isaiah

Isaiah was a prophet in Judah during the reigns of four kings, and his primary message was to warn each king of the threat posed by Assyria and Babylon. But in the middle of these dire threats of judgment, he also gives a message of future hope, looking beyond the immediate future and into the reign of the coming Messiah. This is one of the most beautifully written books of the Bible, filled with powerful images and memorable phrases.

Day 199   Read Isaiah 1–4

Day 200   Read Isaiah 5–8

Day 201   Read Isaiah 9–12

Day 202   Read Isaiah 13–16

Day 203   Read Isaiah 17–21

Day 204　Read Isaiah 22–25

Day 205　Read Isaiah 26–28

Day 206   Read Isaiah 29–31

Day 207   Read Isaiah 32–35

Day 208   Read Isaiah 36–38

Day 209   Read Isaiah 39–42

Day 210   Read Isaiah 43–47

Day 211   Read Isaiah 48–51

Day 212   Read Isaiah 52–56

Day 213   Read Isaiah 57–59

Day 214   Read Isaiah 60–63

Day 215   Read Isaiah 64–66

Introduction to the Book of Jeremiah

Poor Jeremiah! He preached, but no one seemed to be listening. He prophesied in Jerusalem, warning of the impending punishment of Judah, and is known as the "weeping prophet" for the emotional tone of his dire predictions and because of the great sacrifices he made to deliver his message. Throughout his entire career, Jeremiah received no positive response, as though he was preaching into the wind. But he persevered in the face of frustration and pointed toward the Potter (God), who wished to shape the clay (His people) into something beautiful.

Day 216   Read Jeremiah 1–3

Day 217   Read Jeremiah 4–6

Day 218   Read Jeremiah 7–9

Day 219   Read Jeremiah 10–12

Day 220   Read Jeremiah 13–15

Day 221   Read Jeremiah 16–18

Day 222   Read Jeremiah 19–22

Day 223   Read Jeremiah 23–25

Day 224   Read Jeremiah 26–27

Day 225   Read Jeremiah 28–30

Day 226   Read Jeremiah 31–32

Day 227   Read Jeremiah 33–35

Day 228   Read Jeremiah 36–38

Day 229   Read Jeremiah 39–41

Day 230   Read Jeremiah 42–44

Day 231   Read Jeremiah 45–48

Day 232   Read Jeremiah 49–50

Introduction to the Book of Lamentations

Traditionally ascribed to Jeremiah, Lamentations is a book filled with the cries of physical and spiritual agony brought on by the consequences of sin and abandoning God's ways. At the time it was written, Jerusalem lay in ruins at the hands of its enemies. Much of the book, set out as an elaborate acrostic in Hebrew, is a prayer of lament, both calling upon the people to repent and upon God to forgive and vindicate His people against their enemies. A cry of despair over misfortune and suffering is a valid form of prayer!

Day 234   Read Lamentations 1–2

Day 235   Read Lamentations 3–5

Introduction to the Book of Ezekiel

Ezekiel was God's "performance artist." It wasn't enough for him to preach to the exiles in Babylon; he was given the job of enacting a series of odd parables to help his fellow Israelites see the truth and look forward to God's salvation. He ate a scroll—yes, ate it. He lay on his side for 390 days. Then on his other side for many more days. Ezekiel ate only one meal a day...cooked over manure. He smashed pottery and spoke of the fantastical symbolic visions that God had given him. To many, Ezekiel might have seemed crazy, but his message was one of visionary hope.

Day 236   Read Ezekiel 1–4

Day 237   Read Ezekiel 5–8

Day 238   Read Ezekiel 9–12

Day 239   Read Ezekiel 13–15

Day 240   Read Ezekiel 16–19

Day 241   Read Ezekiel 20–21

Day 242   Read Ezekiel 22–23

Day 243   Read Ezekiel 24–26

Day 244   Read Ezekiel 27–28

Day 245   Read Ezekiel 29–31

Day 246   Read Ezekiel 32–33

Day 247 Read Ezekiel 34–36

Day 248 Read Ezekiel 37–38

Day 249   Read Ezekiel 39–40

Day 250   Read Ezekiel 41–43

Day 251   Read Ezekiel 44–45

Day 252   Read Ezekiel 46–48

Introduction to the Book of Daniel

Daniel contains some of the most fascinating stories in all the books of the prophets, as well as some of the most head-scratching prophetic visions. The book is a testament to strong faith in action with prophetic warnings about the future. Daniel was an exiled Jew living in Babylon who resisted the temptation to accommodate a pagan culture. His wisdom and godly character earned him respect and favor.

Day 253   Read Daniel 1–2

Day 254   Read Daniel 3–4

Day 255   Read Daniel 5–7

Day 256 Read Daniel 8–10

Day 257 Read Daniel 11–12

Introduction to the Book of Hosea

The story of the prophet Hosea is a lived-out illustration of God's infinite patience and love for His people. Hosea, a prophet in Israel, is commanded to do something very unexpected and scandalous: marry a known prostitute and have children with her. He does, but the marriage quickly deteriorates due to her unfaithfulness—an unfaithfulness that parallels Israel's unfaithfulness to God. But Hosea does not give up on his wife. His patient love is a reminder of how God feels about His people. Still, there is room for a stern rebuke for their sin. Love sometimes means calling for repentance.

Day 258   Read Hosea 1–5

Day 259 Read Hosea 6–10

Day 260 Read Hosea 11–14

Introduction to the Book of Joel

The prophet Joel's message is that judgment precedes revival. When a plague of locusts descends upon Judah, Joel explains that this is just a foretaste of the coming Day of the Lord when great judgment will come upon all people...unless they humble themselves and repent.

Day 261   Read Joel 1–3

Introduction to the Book of Amos

Amos was a plain-spoken shepherd who, though his home was in Judah, crossed over into Israel to preach. He had strong words of condemnation for Israel's smug, self-satisfied religiosity and their flirtation with idolatry. God, Amos declared, hates false religion. Amos also spoke out against the corruption of Jewish society and the injustice that left the poor forgotten and oppressed. God, he reminded the people, will not tolerate such neglect.

Day 262   Read Amos 1–5

Introduction to the Book of Obadiah

Obadiah is the shortest book in the Old Testament—only one chapter long. Its theme is the coming destruction of Edom (a neighboring nation) due to its wickedness and cruelty. Scholars are not sure where it fits into the chronology of Jewish history, but it seems likely that Obadiah was a contemporary of Elisha.

Introduction to the Book of Jonah

The story of Jonah and the big fish (the Bible doesn't say that it was a whale!) is one of the most familiar Bible stories, but there is more to this book than just that tale. It also provides us with the message that God's love extends beyond His chosen people to encompass all humankind. This book reveals human stubbornness (as seen in Jonah himself) and God's mercy.

Day 264   Read Obadiah and Jonah 1–4

Introduction to the Book of Micah

The prophet Micah speaks out against the social injustice in Israel and Samaria. He points to the oppression of the poor by the rich, the hypocrisy of the national and religious leaders, and the general spiritual bankruptcy of the people. God desires more than just personal holiness. He also demands social righteousness and justice. To that end, Micah gives a prophetic glimpse of the glorious future when the Lord will regather His people in a kingdom ruled by the Messiah.

Day 265   Read Micah 1–2

Introduction to the Book of Nahum

A contemporary of Jeremiah and Zephaniah, Nahum predicts the judgment of Nineveh (some 125 years after Jonah's missionary trip via the big fish). The people had returned to their old ways. The God who is slow to anger, declares Nahum, has finally had it with Nineveh's (and all of Assyria's) evil ways.

Introduction to the Book of Habakkuk

It was a dark time in Judah. A time of violence and corruption, injustice and neglect, and much suffering. And there, on the horizon, was lurking the invasion by Babylon. In the midst of all this conflict, Habakkuk struggles with the question of why God was allowing this to happen. The form of the book is a conversation between the prophet and the Lord. Habakkuk asks the question, and God's answer is simple: It is a judgment upon the corrupt leaders of Judah. The book ends on a high note, with Habakkuk's beautiful prayer of faith and trust.

Introduction to the Book of Zephaniah

Zephaniah was a distant member of the royal family who prophesied during the early reign of Josiah. He assured the people that Judah would be judged and looked toward the coming Day of the Lord. Since Josiah was one of the good kings, Zephaniah's message appears to have gotten through!

Introduction to the Book of Haggai

Haggai was a Jewish exile who returned to Jerusalem with the second wave of returnees. He found the morale of Jerusalem's citizens to be very low. Life was so difficult that the temple project had been temporarily abandoned. Haggai reminded the people that the temple is more than just a building—it is a sign that the land will be rededicated to God. This meant putting God first so that they would experience His blessings.

Day 270   Read Haggai 1–2

Introduction to the Book of Zechariah

Like his contemporary, Haggai, Zechariah was preaching to the discouraged Jews who had returned from exile in Babylon. But instead of focusing on the present as Haggai was doing, Zechariah shares a series of eight strange visions of the future. There is no scholarly agreement on the precise meaning of these visions, but it is clear that much of it concerns Zechariah's prophetic predictions of the coming Messiah, Jesus. And when he is speaking of this glorious future, he can barely contain his excitement.

Day 271   Read Zechariah 1–5

Day 272   Read Zechariah 6–10

Introduction to the Book of Malachi

Probably the last prophet of Old Testament times, Malachi speaks to those who have returned from exile about staying true to God's ways. In these rough times, it was easy to neglect responsibilities to God and His temple, and to become spiritually stagnant. Beware of falsehood and neglect, he says, and stay true to God and follow His ways.

Introduction to the Gospel of Matthew

Matthew is the first of the four Gospels, though it most likely was not the first to be written. That distinction belongs to Mark. Matthew, more than the other three Gospels, looks at the life and death of Jesus from a Jewish perspective, connecting these events with the hopes and expectations of the Jews. Thus, Matthew provides a genealogy that demonstrates Jesus' royal heritage as a descendant of King David and tries to connect the events of Jesus' life with the fulfillment of Old Testament prophecies. He quotes the Old Testament to prove that Jesus of Nazareth is the longed-for Messiah, the One who ushers in the kingdom of God.

Day 275   Read Matthew 1–4

Day 276   Read Matthew 5–6

Day 277   Read Matthew 7–9

Day 278   Read Matthew 10–12

Day 279   Read Matthew 13–14

The Holy Land in the Time of Jesus

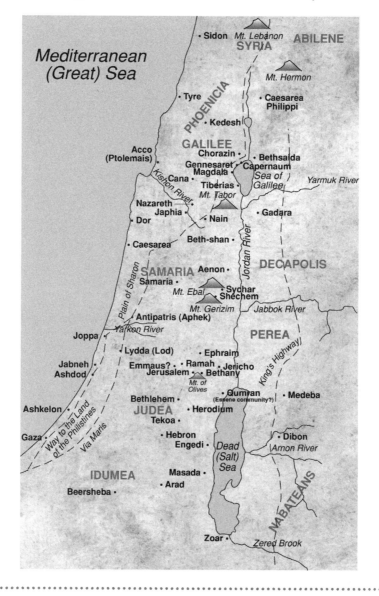

Day 280   Read Matthew 15–17

Day 281   Read Matthew 18–20

Day 282   Read Matthew 21–22

Day 283   Read Matthew 23–24

Day 284   Read Matthew 25–26

Day 285   Read Matthew 27–28

Introduction to the Gospel of Mark

Mark is the earliest of the Gospels, and it is also the shortest and fastest paced. Mark doesn't worry about explaining Jesus' lineage or the details of His birth. He just jumps right into His story, recounting the ministry of Jesus during the three years before His death. Amid all the action, though, Mark stops now and then to explain various Jewish customs that pertain to the story, which leads us to believe that he is writing for a non-Jewish audience, probably Roman citizens. The Romans always loved a man of action, and Jesus was surely such a man.

Day 286   Read Mark 1–3

Day 287 Read Mark 4–5

Day 288 Read Mark 6–7

....

Day 289   Read Mark 8–9

....

Day 290   Read Mark 10–11

....

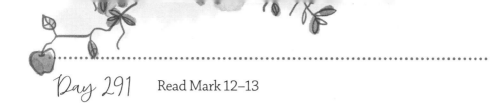

Day 291   Read Mark 12–13

Day 292   Read Mark 14–16

Introduction to the Gospel of Luke

Luke's intentions are made clear in the first few verses of his Gospel: to tell the story of Jesus with an eye for accuracy and research, producing a trustworthy account of what really happened. His audience, as with Mark, was the Gentiles, and Luke was likely a Gentile himself. He recounts the story of the universal Savior, not just for the Jews, but for all people. Luke gives a lot of attention to the teaching of Jesus, particularly the parables. And he shows a deep sympathy with Jesus' concern for the outcasts of society: the poor, the downtrodden, the sick, and the suffering. To them Jesus brings a message of hope and the love of a heavenly Father.

Day 293   Read Luke 1–3

Day 294   Read Luke 4–5

Day 295   Read Luke 6–7

Day 296   Read Luke 8–9

Day 297   Read Luke 10–11

Day 298   Read Luke 12–13

Day 299   Read Luke 14–16

Day 300   Read Luke 17–18

Day 301   Read Luke 19–20

Day 302   Read Luke 21–22

Day 303   Read Luke 23–24

Introduction to the Gospel of John

The first three Gospels are often referred to as the "Synoptic Gospels" due to the similarities in the events they portray. John's Gospel is different than the others. More philosophical and theological, it explores the deepest mysteries of who Jesus was and why He came. The book is structured around the great signs of Jesus' divinity and the "I am" statements that Jesus utters. In many ways, it is the most personally moving and spiritually challenging of the Gospels and focuses on many memorable monologues given by Jesus.

Day 304   Read John 1–3

Day 305   Read John 4–5

Day 306   Read John 6–7

Day 307   Read John 8–9

Day 308   Read John 10–11

Day 309   Read John 12–13

Day 310   Read John 14–16

THE "I AM" STATEMENTS OF JESUS (FROM THE GOSPEL OF JOHN)

- I am the Bread of Life (John 6:35,48)
- I am the Light of the World (John 8:12; 9:5)
- I am the Door (John 10:7,9)
- I am the Good Shepherd (John 10:11,14)
- I am the Resurrection and the Life (John 11:25)
- I am the Way, the Truth, and the Life (John 14:6)
- I am the True Vine (John 15:1)

Day 311   Read John 17–18

Day 312   Read John 19–21

Introduction to the Book of Acts

In Acts, Luke continues the narrative he began in his Gospel by sharing the story of the early church. He recounts the way the church expanded in an almost concentric manner—first Jerusalem, then Samaria, then to the ends of the earth. For the first twelve chapters, the focus is largely on Peter, though we also see the story of Stephen, the first martyr. One of those present at Stephen's death is a Pharisee named Saul. In chapter 13, the focus of Acts changes to Saul, who is converted and given a new name: Paul. The remainder of Acts deals with Paul's courageous witness throughout the Roman world to Jews and Gentiles alike.

Day 313   Read Acts 1–3

Day 314   Read Acts 4–6

Day 315   Read Acts 7–8

Day 316   Read Acts 9–10

Day 317   Read Acts 11–13

Paul's Missionary Journeys

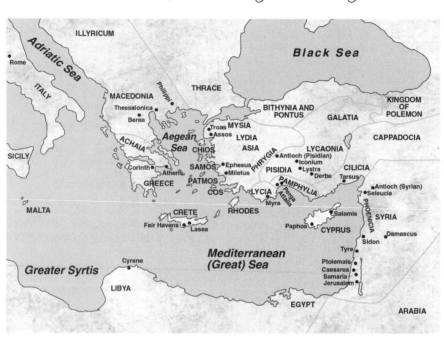

First Missionary Journey:

Cyprus, Perga, Pisidian Antioch, Iconium, Lystra, and Derbe (13:2–14:28)

Second Missionary Journey:

Troas, Philippi, Thessalonica, Berea, Athens, Corinth, and Ephesus (15:36–18:22)

Third Missionary Journey:

Ephesus, Troas, and Miletus (19:22–21:16)

Day 318   Read Acts 14–16

Day 319   Read Acts 17–18

Day 320   Read Acts 19–20

Day 321   Read Acts 21–22

Day 322   Read Acts 23–25

Day 323   Read Acts 26–28

Introduction to the Letter to the Romans

More than any other of Paul's letters, Romans is the New Testament's theology book. This letter, written to the Christians in Rome, is Paul's attempt to explain the meaning of the Gospel—that salvation is not the result of efforts or moral goodness, but solely based upon what Jesus has accomplished through His death and resurrection. The message is, We are all guilty, but Jesus has become the "New Adam" and made a way for us to be restored to a relationship with God—a relationship so intimate that we may call Him *Father*. Nothing, Paul reminds us, can sever us from God's love.

Day 324   Read Romans 1–3

Day 325   Read Romans 4–7

Day 326   Read Romans 8–10

Day 327   Read Romans 11–14

Day 328   Read Romans 15–16

Introduction to the First Letter to the Corinthians

The church at Corinth had a lot of problems...and they are problems that sound familiar to us even today. It was a church marked by division, enmity and infighting, sexual immorality, an unwillingness to live by God's commands, and taking worship (especially the Lord's Supper) too lightly. Paul points out that there are two kinds of Christians: the spiritual, who live by the power of God's indwelling Spirit, and the worldly, who simply live by their own desires. To find true unity, meaningful worship, and moral strength, Paul reminds the Corinthians that we are all interconnected and differently gifted members of the body of Christ.

Day 329   Read 1 Corinthians 1–4

....

Day 330   Read 1 Corinthians 5–8

....

Day 331   Read 1 Corinthians 9–11

....

Day 332   Read 1 Corinthians 12–14

Day 333   Read 1 Corinthians 15–16

Introduction to the Second Letter to the Corinthians

Some of the recipients of Paul's earlier letter to Corinth had taken a "who are you to tell us what to do?" attitude toward the apostle. In this second letter, Paul defends his life and ministry, pointing to the way that God had honored the call upon his life with great success and fruitfulness. Speaking from experience, Paul also points out that the life of service to God can sometimes result in great suffering and persecution.

Day 334   Read 2 Corinthians 1–4

Day 335   Read 2 Corinthians 5–8

Day 336   Read 2 Corinthians 9–13

Introduction to the Letter to the Galatians

Probably the earliest of Paul's letters, this letter deals with one of the thorniest issues to face the early church: religious legalism. Because the church arose out of Judaism, should Gentile believers be required to follow the Jewish laws and, specifically, the rite of circumcision? Paul's answer is clear and stated strongly: No. He asserts that the gospel of Jesus is not about laws and good works, but about faith and love. Through grace, he says, Christ has made us free.

Day 337   Read Galatians 1–3

Introduction to the Letter to the Ephesians

Paul's letter to the Ephesians reminds the Christian that we are chosen and loved by God, but also empowered by the Spirit to live a new life in Christ. That new life is manifested in a holy lifestyle, our family relationships, and in our ability to withstand the temptations of the devil, the enemy of our souls. The letter has two neatly divided halves—the first section provides a theological understanding of how we are empowered to live as Christians, and the second gives us practical instructions for "walking in the Spirit."

Day 339   Read Ephesians 1–3

Day 340   Read Ephesians 4–6

Introduction to the Letter to the Philippians

Philippians can be best understood as a thank-you note from Paul. While he was under house arrest, the church at Philippi had not forgotten him and had sent him a gift. He expresses his appreciation and urges them to continue in the way they have begun—following Jesus with faithfulness and joy. Paul himself was an example of being joyful no matter what the circumstances.

Day 341   Read Philippians 1–4

Introduction to the Letter to the Colossians

For some people, the simplicity of the gospel is too simple! They want to find ways to make it more complicated, more intellectually exclusive. When Paul heard that such tendencies were a problem in Colossae, he sent a letter warning against an overly intellectualized approach to faith. The Colossians had grafted a lot of mystical concepts and dietary laws onto the gospel. Paul provides them with a strong reminder that Christianity is all about Christ...and Christ alone.

Day 342

Read Colossians 1–4

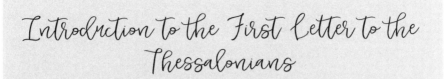

Introduction to the First Letter to the Thessalonians

This letter has a more positive tone than most of Paul's letters. He finds much to commend in the church at Thessalonica: their missionary zeal, their dedication to the truth, and their conduct in the world. Lest they become discouraged in the face of mounting persecution, Paul reminds them of a blessed hope: Jesus is coming again!

Day 343   Read 1 Thessalonians 1–5

Introduction to the Second Letter to the Thessalonians

As in his earlier letter, Paul comforts the Thessalonians with a reminder of Christ's promised return. However, he has to clear up some misunderstandings about that event because many Christians, expecting the imminent return of Jesus, had neglected to continue working to earn a living. They had built their life around waiting for the Second Coming rather than staying focused on doing the work of God. Maybe this is a healthy reminder for those who put too much emphasis on the study of Bible prophecy.

Day 344   Read 2 Thessalonians 1–3

Introduction to the First and Second Letters to Timothy

These two letters are addressed from Paul to a young church leader named Timothy. The pride Paul feels in his protégé is very clear, but that doesn't stop him from offering a good deal of advice and instruction on how to be a better pastor to his flock. By the time he writes the second letter—probably Paul's last—the relationship seems even closer, and Paul encourages Timothy to "finish the race."

Day 345   Read 1 Timothy 1–3

Day 346   Read 1 Timothy 4–6

Day 347   Read 2 Timothy 1–4

Introduction to the Letter to Titus

Like Timothy, Titus was a young church leader whom Paul encourages and instructs. In this letter, he writes about very specific guidelines regarding qualifications of church leadership and the conduct of the church. His two key themes are the primacy of moral character and the importance of sound doctrine.

Introduction to the Letter to Philemon

Onesimus was a slave in Colossae who escaped from his master, Philemon, and made his way to Rome. There in Rome he became a Christian through the ministry of Paul. Interestingly, Philemon had been tutored in the faith by Paul some years earlier. So Paul writes a short personal letter asking him to forgive Onesimus and accept him back as a brother in Christ.

Introduction to the Letter to the Hebrews

So...how does Christianity fit into the rich heritage of Judaism? That's the topic of this letter to Hebrew Christians. Its author (probably not Paul because the style of this letter is radically different from Paul's other correspondence) argues that Christianity is the fulfillment of Judaism. Reviewing Old Testament history, the author demonstrates that everything in Jewish tradition—priesthood, sacrifices, covenant, the Law—points forward to a rich fulfillment in Jesus Christ and His work as the superior Priest and Prophet.

Day 349   Read Hebrews 1–3

Day 350   Read Hebrews 4–6

Day 351   Read Hebrews 7–9

Day 352   Read Hebrews 10–11

Introduction to the Letter of James

If salvation comes through grace and faith, then where do good works fit in? That is the question posed and answered in this letter by James, the brother of Jesus. Because he believes that good works are the natural outgrowth of an authentic faith, this letter is filled with practical advice about how to put faith into action. James helps believers think about how their faith is related to the way they talk, the way they spend their money, and the way they relate to the world around them.

Introduction to the First and Second Letters of Peter

Suffering is a universal part of the human experience. And it was a very immediate reality to the early Christians, who were often severely persecuted for their faith. The author of these two letters, the apostle Peter, certainly knew suffering firsthand and eventually gave his life for the cause of the gospel. In the first letter, he encourages Christians to hang on to their faith, despite the difficulties, and promises that suffering is a prelude to glory. In the second letter, Peter points toward the hope Christians can have because Jesus is coming again.

Day 355   Read 1 Peter 1–5

Day 356   Read 2 Peter 1–3

Introduction to the First, Second, and Third Letters of John

These three letters from the apostle John are written to counter a major threat to early Christianity—the teachings of the Gnostics, a sect that challenged the orthodox view of who Jesus was and how Christians should live out their faith in Him. The Gnostic view of sin was such that they felt the actions of the body really didn't matter. John argues that a pure life is of utmost importance and that love is the primary sign of a vibrant faith.

Day 357   Read 1 John 1–5

Introduction to the Letter of Jude

Jude, written by a brother of James and Jesus, is another letter emphasizing the importance of correct doctrine. He challenged the false teachings that were making their way into the church and called believers to live in the holiness that finds its foundation in a true faith.

Day 358   Read 2 John, 3 John, and Jude

Introduction to the Book of Revelation

Some Christians spend more time studying Revelation than just about any other book of the Bible. Others neglect it almost entirely, considering it puzzling and confusing. There is no question that it contains some of the most difficult and obscure passages in all of Scripture. Therefore, it should come as no surprise that Christians continue to argue about its correct interpretation. What is clear is that the book contains the visions given to John while in exile on the island of Patmos, and that these visions are cloaked in very poetic and symbolic language.

Day 359   Read Revelation 1–3

A FEW THOUGHTS ON INTERPRETING REVELATION

Some see this book as a prophecy of the future events of the last days. Others see it as a symbolic picture of the struggles of the church in an age of intense suffering at the hands of the Roman Empire. Some would say that most of the events of the book lie in the future, while others think that it is symbolic reading of much that has already occurred. Perhaps all can agree on this much: In many ways, Revelation is a fifth Gospel, John's portrayal of the risen Jesus (the Lamb), who will eventually conquer all the powers of evil that oppose God's kingdom. That was a comforting message to the readers of its time and is to us today. In the book of Revelation, we see how the story will end: with the triumph of God over all manner of evil, and the creation of a new heaven and a new earth.

Day 360   Read Revelation 4–7

Day 361   Read Revelation 8–11

Day 362   Read Revelation 12–15

Day 363   Read Revelation 16–18

Day 364   Read Revelation 19–20

Congratulations!

I hope you have enjoyed this journey through the Bible and that it has both challenged and inspired you. I also hope that this year of reading has developed a new habit and that you will continue reading the Bible daily, for it is a book that is old, but ever new. I've found that each rereading of the Bible brings new insights and new inspirations, as new understandings open up before my eyes. It is a companion for life. Ready to start over again at the beginning?

notes

notes

notes

notes

notes

notes

notes